Family

Rebecca Rissman

Raintree

Raintree is an imprint of Capstone Global Library Limited, a company incorporated in England and Wales having its registered office at 7 Pilgrim Street, London, EC4V 6LB – Registered company number: 6695582

www.raintreepublishers.co.uk
myorders@raintreepublishers.co.uk

Text © Capstone Global Library Limited 2013
First published in hardback in 2013
Paperback edition first published in 2014
The moral rights of the proprietor have been asserted.

Edited by Rebecca Rissman, Daniel Nunn, and
 Catherine Veitch
Designed by Philippa Jenkins
Picture research by Ruth Blair
Production by Victoria Fitzgerald
Originated by Capstone Global Library
Printed and bound in China

ISBN 978 1 406 25142 5 (hardback)
16 15 14 13 12
10 9 8 7 6 5 4 3 2 1

ISBN 978 1 406 25147 0 (paperback)
18 17 16 15 14
10 9 8 7 6 5 4 3 2 1

British Library Cataloguing in Publication Data
Rissman, Rebecca.
Family. -- (Say What You See!)
306.8'5-dc23
A full catalogue record for this book is available from the British Library.

Acknowledgements
We would like to thank the following for permission to reproduce photographs: iStockphoto pp. 13 (© Pavel Losevsky), 16 (© kristian sekulic), 20 (© Chuck Schmidt); Shutterstock pp. title page (© Rob Marmion), 4 (© privilege), 5 (© wavebreakmedia ltd, © Monkey Business Images), 6 (© Kzenon), 7 (© wavebreakmedia ltd, © Rob Marmion, © Yuri Arcurs), 8 (© IrinaK, © Anatoliy Samara), 9 (© Monkey Business Images), 10 (© Monkey Business Images), 11 (© Gemenacom, © Monkey Business Images), 12 (© Karen Struthers), 13 (© Monkey Business Images), 14 (© wavebreakmedia ltd), 15 (© Dmitriy Shironosov, © Monkey Business Images, © BlueOrange Studio), 16 (© thieury), 17 (© Kruchankova Maya, © Poznyakov), 18 (© Gorilla), 19 (© UbjsP, © Rdaniel), 20 (© Monkey Business Images), 21 (© Andrew L.), 22 (© Monkey Business Images, © Phase4Photography).

Cover photograph of a family reproduced with permission of Shutterstock (© Monkey Business Images).

Every effort has been made to contact copyright holders of material reproduced in this book. Any omissions will be rectified in subsequent printings if notice is given to the publisher.

Contents

What are these
families doing? 4

Can you find these
things in the book? 23

Index 24

What are these families doing?
Say what you see!

Talking

Cooking

Eating

Playing

Puzzling

Cleaning

Washing

Gardening

Watering

Building

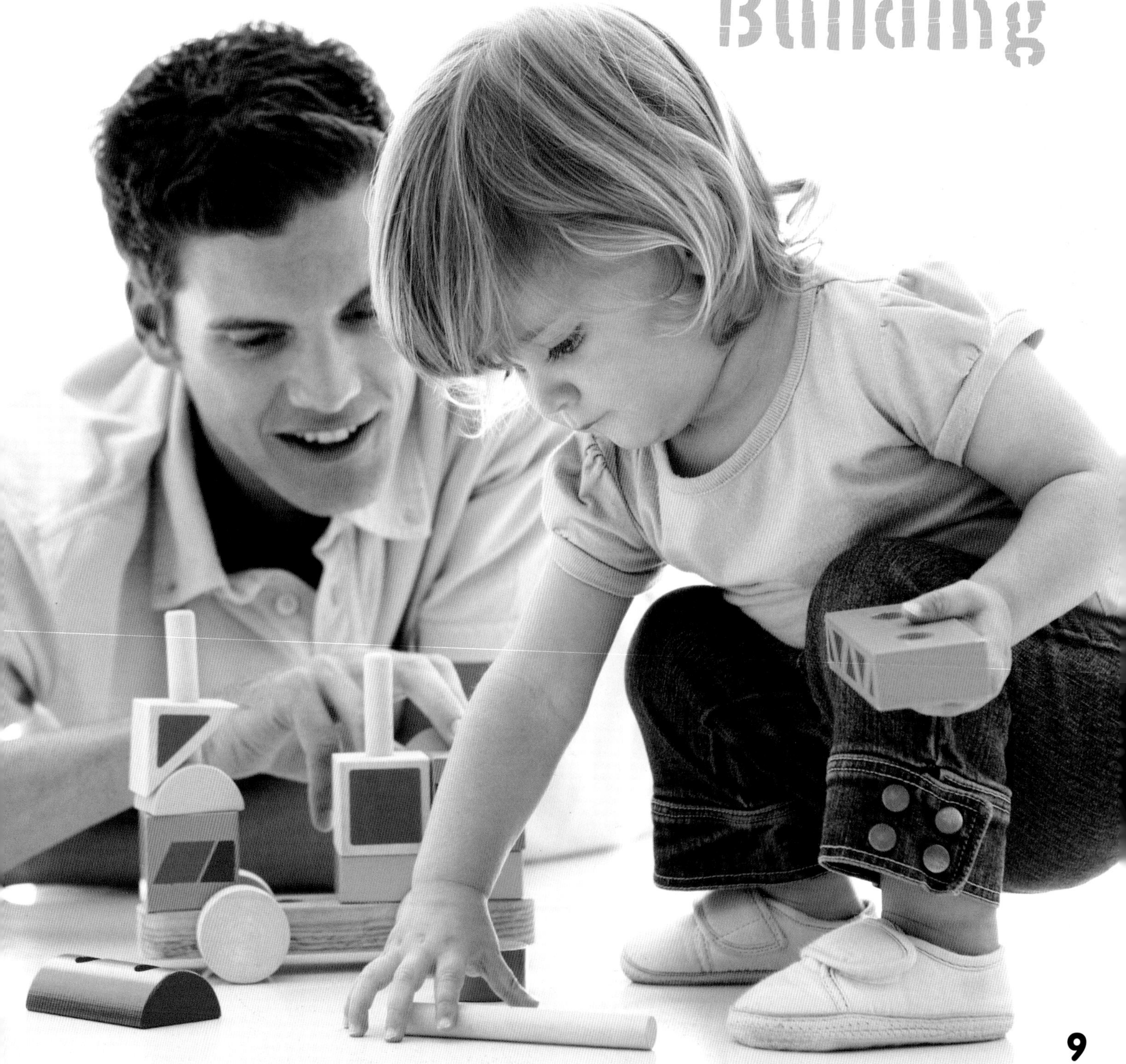

Driving

Riding

Walking

Running

Reading

Being Silly

Learning

Watching

Travelling

Splashing

Sightseeing

Rushing

Relaxing

Painting

Creating

17

Racing

Throwing

Skating

Sharing

Caring

Arguing

21

Hugging

Laughing

Can you find these things in the book? Look back... and say what you see!

riding

washing

building

caring

Index

ball 6
bike 10
blocks 9
book 12
car 10
craft 17
food 5, 20
garden 8
ice skates 19

paint 17
paper 17
puzzle 7
sledge 18
snowball 19
soap 7
watering can 8